Things to Know When Interviewing for a CFO Role

Table of Contents

Introduction

The world of finance is constantly evolving and so are the roles of financial leaders within organizations. A Chief Financial Officer (CFO) is a strategic leader who plays a vital role in decision-making and financial planning for a company. However, it is not easy to land a CFO job as it is a highly competitive position that requires a combination of skills and experience.

For those looking to interview for a CFO role, it is important to have a solid understanding of the key terminologies used in the job function. Being familiar with these terms not only helps in being more confident during the interview but also equips you with the knowledge to ask better questions and understand the company's financial goals more effectively. This book aims to provide a comprehensive glossary of terms related to finance and accounting, which will be helpful for anyone looking to land a CFO role.

Accounting Principles

A set of guidelines and standards governing the preparation of financial statements. As a CFO, understanding the accounting principles is essential to ensure accurate and reliable financial reporting.

Accounting Standards Board

An organization that creates and enforces accounting standards in a specific country or region. As a CFO, it is crucial to keep up-to-date with changes in accounting standards as it affects financial reporting and compliance.

Accounts Payable

Money owed by a company to its suppliers or vendors. As a CFO, managing accounts payable is important for cash management and maintaining good relationships with suppliers.

Accounts Receivable

Money owed to a company from its customers. As a CFO, managing accounts receivable is vital as it affects cash flows and liquidity.

Accrual Accounting

A method of accounting that recognizes revenue and expenses when they are incurred, not when they are received or paid. As a CFO, understanding the mechanics of accrual accounting is crucial as it affects the timing of financial reporting.

Amortization

The process of reducing the value of an intangible asset over a specific period. As a CFO, understanding the concept of amortization is critical as it affects the financial statements and tax reporting.

Annual Budget

A financial plan outlining expected income and expenses for the upcoming year. As a CFO, preparing the annual budget is a critical task as it sets financial targets and guides decision-making.

Annual Report

A comprehensive report including the financial statements, notes to the financial statements, and management discussion and analysis. As a CFO, preparing the annual report is an essential part of the job as it portrays the company's financial performance to stakeholders.

Asset Management

The process of managing a company's assets to ensure they are being used effectively to generate maximum returns. As a CFO, managing assets is important for efficient resource utilization and meeting financial objectives.

Audit Committee

A group of independent directors responsible for overseeing the financial reporting process and internal control system. As a CFO, interacting with the audit committee is crucial as they are responsible for ensuring that accurate and reliable financial reporting is done.

Balance Sheet Analysis

Analysis of a company's financial health by assessing its assets, liabilities, and shareholder equity for a specific period. The CFO must be well-versed in interpreting balance sheet data to make sound business decisions.

Banking Relationships

The process by which a company interacts and transacts with its financial institutions. CFOs must develop and maintain strategic relationships with banks and financial institutions, negotiating better terms and conditions for the organization's financial dealings.

Board of Directors

A group of individuals responsible for overseeing the management and strategic direction of the company. CFOs must work closely with the Board of Directors to ensure the company stays compliant with the regulatory frameworks while minimizing risk exposure.

Bottom Line

Refers to a company's net income or profit. During an interview for a CFO role, the candidate's ability to ensure the company's bottom line is both healthy and efficient will be closely scrutinized.

Budgeting

The process of forecasting future financial activities and setting financial goals with the aim of achieving them. CFOs play a crucial role in developing budgets and ensuring the timely allocation of resources in line with organizational goals.

Burn Rate

The rate at which a company spends its available resources, including cash and time. The CFO must carefully monitor the company's burn rate to ensure that it can meet its financial obligations while pursuing its strategic goals.

Business Continuity Planning

A proactive process that ensures the smooth running of a company's critical operations during a crisis or natural disaster. CFOs must facilitate and participate in an effective business continuity planning process that guarantees the company's resilience and longevity.

Business Intelligence

The process of analyzing complex business data to develop actionable insights. CFOs must be well-versed in business intelligence tools and technologies to leverage insights and drive business performance.

Business Model

The process by which a company makes money. During an interview for a CFO role, the right candidate should be able to articulate the company's business model as well as assess and optimize its efficacy.

Business Strategy

A company's plan to achieve its goals and objectives. CFOs must work closely with the leadership team to develop an effective business strategy, monitor its progress and make real-time adjustments where necessary.

Capital Allocation

A term that refers to the process of deciding where a company invests its resources. CFOs play a critical role in capital allocation by determining how much money to allocate to various departments or projects, weighing the potential return on investment against the risk involved.

Capital Markets

A term that refers to the markets where companies can obtain funding by selling securities to investors. CFOs must have a good understanding of capital markets, such as stock exchanges, bond markets, and alternative financing sources, to ensure the company secures funding at the lowest possible cost.

Capital Structure

A term that refers to the mix of debt and equity financing a company uses to fund its operations. CFOs must determine the optimal capital structure to balance the benefits and costs of different financing sources, including interest payments, dividends, and ownership dilution. The capital structure decision has significant implications for a company's financial performance and risk profile.

Cash Flow

A term that refers to the movement of money in and out of a company. Cash flow is crucial for CFOs to monitor as they need to ensure there is enough money to pay expenses, meet short-term obligations, and invest in long-term growth. Positive cash flow occurs when more money is coming in than going out, while negative cash flow indicates a company is spending more money than it is earning.

Compliance

A term that refers to ensuring a company is following all applicable laws and regulations. CFOs are responsible for ensuring corporate compliance with financial and accounting rules, including tax regulations, internal controls, and disclosures to investors.

Contingency Planning

A term that refers to the process of preparing for unexpected events that could negatively impact a company. CFOs must participate in contingency planning to identify potential risks to the business, such as natural disasters, economic downturns, and cybersecurity threats, and develop plans to mitigate those risks.

Corporate Finance

A term that encompasses all financial activities related to running a business, including investments, mergers and acquisitions, and financing decisions. CFOs play a critical role in corporate finance, providing strategic guidance on major financial decisions and ensuring the company maintains a healthy financial position.

Corporate Governance

A term that refers to the system of rules, policies, and practices that govern a company's operations and decision-making processes. CFOs must ensure the company follows sound corporate governance practices to maintain its reputation, attract investors, and reduce potential legal liabilities.

Cost Accounting

A term that refers to the process of tracking and analyzing all costs associated with creating a product or service. CFOs must have a solid understanding of cost accounting to determine the profitability of different products or services and make strategic decisions about pricing, inventory management, and production planning.

Cost of Capital

A term that refers to the price a company pays to obtain funding. The cost of capital takes into account both debt and equity financing, and companies must balance the two to minimize their overall cost of capital. CFOs must carefully manage the cost of capital to ensure the company is not overpaying for funding sources, which can negatively impact profitability.

Debt Financing

A type of financing where a company borrows money from a lender, such as a bank or institutional investor, in exchange for repayment with interest. CFOs must understand the various types of debt financing available, such as lines of credit, term loans, and bonds. They must also negotiate favorable terms and interest rates, and ensure proper documentation and compliance with debt covenants.

Debt-to-Equity Ratio (D/E Ratio)

A financial ratio that compares a company's total debt to its total equity. CFOs use the D/E ratio to assess the company's leverage and financial risk. A high D/E ratio indicates that the company has more debt than equity, which can increase interest payments and reduce the company's ability to withstand financial shocks.

Deficit

A negative balance in a company's earnings, such as a net operating loss or a shortfall in cash flows. CFOs must develop strategies to address deficits and improve the company's financial outlook. This may involve cutting costs, increasing revenue, or seeking financing options.

Derivatives

Financial instruments that derive their value from an underlying asset, such as stocks, bonds, or commodities. CFOs must be knowledgeable about various types of derivatives, such as options and futures, and their risks and benefits. They must also assess the impact of derivatives on the company's financial statements and hedging strategies.

Diluted Earnings Per Share (EPS)

A measure of a company's profitability that takes into account the potential dilution of outstanding shares from stock options, warrants, and convertible securities. CFOs must accurately calculate diluted EPS to provide a full view of the company's financial performance and inform capital-raising decisions.

Disclosure

The presentation of information about a company's financial performance and operations to stakeholders, such as investors and regulators. CFOs must ensure that all required disclosures are accurate, timely, and transparent. Failure to disclose material information can result in legal liability and damage to the company's reputation.

Discounted Cash Flow (DCF)

A valuation method used to estimate the intrinsic value of a company by forecasting future cash flows and discounting them back to their present value. CFOs must be proficient in DCF modeling to make informed investment decisions and communicate financial projections to stakeholders.

Divestiture

The process of selling or spinning off a portion of a company's business or assets. CFOs must determine the financial benefits and risks of divestiture, including potential tax implications and the impact on the company's financial statements. They must also manage the transaction process and communicate effectively with stakeholders.

Dividend Policy

A strategy for distributing profits to shareholders through regular dividend payments. CFOs must develop and implement a sound dividend policy that strikes a balance between investor expectations and the company's financial goals. They must also consider the tax implications and the impact of dividend payments on the company's cash flow.

Due Diligence

A comprehensive review of a company's financial and legal records to ensure accuracy and compliance. CFOs must perform thorough due diligence before any merger or acquisition to assess the financial risks and liabilities involved. Due diligence also includes identifying potential tax liabilities, debts, and contractual obligations that may impact the financial health of the company.

Earnings per Share

A widely used financial metric calculated by dividing a company's net income by the average number of shares outstanding. CFOs use the calculation of earnings per share to help them make key financial decisions such as determining share price and deciding whether to distribute profits to shareholders by means of dividend payments.

Ebitda

Earnings Before Interest, Taxes, Depreciation, and Amortization (EBITDA) is a financial metric used to measure a company's operating performance. CFOs routinely use EBITDA in presentations to investors and lenders as it helps to give an accurate picture of the company's profitability and financial health.

Enterprise Risk Management

A framework used by CFOs to identify and assess the risks associated with their business strategy and operations. CFOs need to ensure that the risks are managed effectively, thus minimizing the impact of any adverse events on the company's operations or financial performance.

Enterprise Value

Enterprise Value (EV) is the total value of a company's equity, debt, and cash, used by CFOs in calculating the takeover value of their organization. The EV metric helps CFOs assess a company's worth and its investment potential with potential buyers.

Equity

Equity refers to the ownership interest in the company, represented by common and preferred stock. CFOs need to calculate and manage the equity structure of the organization to ensure compliance with regulatory requirements and to optimize the capital structure.

ERP

An enterprise resource planning (ERP) system is a software used by a CFO to manage and integrate different business functions such as finance, accounting, HR, and supply chain. It provides real-time data to enable CFOs to make strategic decisions about finance and resource allocation across the organization.

ESG

Environmental, Social, and Governance (ESG) criteria represent standards for sustainability and ethical practices in the investment community. CFOs need to consider ESG factors in their investment strategy, including risk management and regulatory compliance, to ensure that their organization aligns with global practices and emerging stakeholder expectations.

ETF

An Exchange-Traded Fund (ETF) is a type of investment fund traded on stock exchanges like individual stocks. CFOs increasingly use ETFs as a means to diversify their company's portfolio, manage risk and improve profitability.

Executive Compensation

Executive compensation refers to the compensation package that senior managers receive including salaries, bonuses, share options, and other incentives. Chief financial officers are responsible for designing and implementing executive compensation programs in their organizations that incentivize managers to perform and align with the company's long-term goals.

Expense Ratio

An expense ratio is a measure of the cost of managing an investment portfolio, expressed as a percentage of the assets under management. For a CFO, expense ratios are important in selecting the right investment portfolio for their organization, closely monitoring investment performance, and reporting to investors on the funds' efficacy and cost-effectiveness.

Financial Analysis

Financial analysis involves using quantitative methods to evaluate a company's financial performance. A CFO should have a strong background in financial analysis, including the use of financial ratios, trend analysis, and other financial metrics to assess a company's profitability, liquidity, and overall financial health.

Financial Controls

Financial controls are processes and procedures put in place to safeguard a company's financial assets and resources. A CFO should be familiar with different financial controls, such as internal audits, financial reporting policies, and fraud prevention strategies.

Financial Planning

Financial planning involves developing and implementing a long-term financial strategy for a company. A CFO should be able to create financial plans that align with the company's overall goals and objectives, and ensure that the company is on track to meet its financial targets.

Financial Reporting

Financial reporting involves preparing and delivering financial information to stakeholders, including investors, regulators, and company management. As a CFO, you should be responsible for ensuring that financial reports are accurate, timely, and in compliance with regulatory requirements. You should be familiar with different financial reporting standards and be able to communicate financial information effectively to different audiences.

Financial Statements

A financial statement is a document that provides an overview of a company's financial performance. When interviewing for a CFO role, you should have a strong understanding of the different financial statements, including the income statement, balance sheet, and cash flow statement. You should be able to discuss how these statements are prepared and their significance as a measure of a company's financial health.

Financial Strategy

Financial strategy involves developing and implementing a plan to achieve the company's long-term financial goals. A CFO should have experience in financial strategy development, including creating financial models to predict future revenue and profit, developing budgets and financial forecasts, and identifying key areas for investment and growth.

Fiscal Oversight

Fiscal oversight involves monitoring the financial operations of a company to ensure that budgets are met, expenses are controlled, and financial risks are managed effectively. As a CFO, you should have experience in fiscal oversight, including developing and implementing financial policies and procedures to ensure that the company is operating efficiently and effectively.

Forecasting

Forecasting is the process of predicting future financial performance based on past trends and current data. A CFO should have experience in forecasting revenue and expenses, as well as creating financial models that can be used to predict future cash flow and profitability.

Fraud Detection

Fraud detection refers to the process of identifying and preventing fraudulent activity within a company. As a CFO, you should be able to implement fraud detection measures to prevent financial losses and protect the company's reputation.

Fundraising

Fundraising involves securing new sources of funding to support the company's growth and operations. A CFO should have experience in fundraising, including finding sources of debt and equity financing, negotiating deals with investors, and managing relationships with stakeholders.

Gap Analysis

An analysis that compares actual performance to expected performance to identify areas of improvement. As CFO, conducting gap analyses can help identify areas where financial performance can be improved.

Going Concern

A term used to describe whether or not a company is likely to continue its operations in the foreseeable future. As CFO, you must regularly assess and report on the company's going concern status to stakeholders.

Goodwill

Refers to intangible assets such as brand recognition, customer loyalty, and reputation that can contribute to a company's overall value. As CFO, you must understand the value and potential risks associated with your company's goodwill.

Governance

Refers to the system of rules, practices, and processes by which a company is directed and controlled. As CFO, you are responsible for ensuring that the company operates within the bounds of its governance framework.

Green Bonds

A financial instrument that is used to raise funds specifically for environmental projects or initiatives. As CFO, managing and promoting green bonds can be a way to increase interest in your company and demonstrate your commitment to sustainability.

Gross Margin

Represents the difference between the revenue generated by a company and the cost of production or goods sold. As CFO, it is important to monitor gross margin, as it can provide insight into a company's profitability and financial health.

Group Reporting

Refers to the process of consolidating financial data from multiple entities within a group of companies. As CFO, it can be your responsibility to ensure accurate and timely group reporting, which can provide invaluable insight into overall financial performance.

Growth Metrics

Various metrics that are used to gauge or measure the growth of a company. Some common growth metrics may include revenue growth, customer acquisition or retention rates, and expansion into new markets. It is essential for CFOs to identify and monitor growth metrics to help guide strategic decision-making.

Growth-oriented strategies

Various strategies that companies can use to achieve growth targets such as mergers and acquisitions, expanding into new markets, or increasing marketing efforts. CFOs may play a critical role in selecting and executing growth-oriented strategies.

GAAP

Generally accepted accounting principles. These are guidelines that all companies must follow when reporting their financial information. As a CFO, it is important to have a thorough understanding of GAAP to ensure accurate financial reporting and compliance with regulations.

Health benefits

Employee benefits related to healthcare, such as medical, dental, and vision insurance. CFOs must be knowledgeable about different health benefit plans and their costs in order to make informed decisions that balance employee needs and company budget constraints.

Hedging strategy

A method of reducing risk in the financial markets by taking a position that offsets potential losses. CFOs need to understand hedging strategies and be able to implement them effectively to protect company assets against currency, commodity, or interest rate fluctuations.

High-yield debt

Debt instruments that offer high interest rates to compensate for higher risk. CFOs must be able to assess the risk and cost of high-yield debt offerings when considering capital raising options for their company.

Hiring metrics

Key data points that a CFO should be aware of when hiring new staff for their team. These metrics may include time-to-hire, cost-to-hire, and quality-of-hire. It is important for the CFO to track these metrics to optimize the hiring process and ensure that only qualified candidates are brought on board.

Historical financial statements

Reports summarizing a company's financial performance over past accounting periods. CFOs must have a thorough understanding of these statements to be able to analyze trends and make informed decisions about future financial planning.

Human resources compliance

Regulatory requirements governing a company's employment practices, such as equal opportunity, anti-discrimination, and worker safety laws. CFOs must ensure that the company is compliant with all applicable regulations to avoid costly penalties and lawsuits.

Hypothetical scenarios

Simulation exercises used to model potential future outcomes under different economic, market, or operational conditions. CFOs must be able to analyze and interpret the results of hypothetical scenarios to plan for contingencies and inform decision-making.

IFRS

Stands for International Financial Reporting Standards. These standards are critical for companies operating or planning to operate in the global market because it ensures that financial statements produced follow a set of standards that are accepted worldwide. CFOs must be well-versed in IFRS to prepare accurate financial statements for international transactions.

Implicit cost

An implicit cost is an opportunity cost that arises when an activity forgone alternatives. For example, a CFO may face an implicit cost when they choose to invest in long-term development projects rather than using the funds for short-term cash management. Being aware of implicit costs is an essential part of strategic financial planning.

Income statement

CFOs are responsible for preparing the company's income statement, which displays revenues, expenses, and profit or loss for a specific period. A precise income statement will provide the company with insights into its profitability and cash flow situation, making it a crucial tool in the decision-making process.

Insurance

CFOs play a critical role in managing the company's insurance program, including the purchase of insurance policies that mitigate potential risks. They must identify the risks inherent to the organization and select appropriate insurance coverage that protects those risks.

Interest rate

CFOs must stay up-to-date with the fluctuating interest rates, as it affects the company's financial operations. They must assess how interest rates may impact borrowing, investing, and financial strategic planning, leading to better decision-making.

Internal controls

Effective internal controls are critical for CFOs to ensure that financial statements are reliable, assets are protected, and the organization complies with relevant laws and regulations. Internal controls include procedures, policies, and systems that help the organization operate efficiently while mitigating risk. These controls also help provide assurance to stakeholders that the financial statements are accurate.

Internal reporting

CFOs must communicate the company's financial information and insights to internal stakeholders across various departments. This includes board members, executives, and other top-level management to make informed decisions that propel the company forward. Effective internal reporting systems also help facilitate meaningful performance measurement and evaluation.

Inventory management

CFOs play a crucial role in managing inventory levels and reporting inventory-related data to other departments to ensure uninterrupted business operations. Proper inventory management will maintain a balance between carrying too little inventory (leading to stockouts and unhappy customers) or carrying too much (increased holding costs and obsolete remaining stock).

Investor relations

CFOs often serve as the primary point of contact for investors and analysts. They must be adept in communicating the company's financial performance and strategy clearly, transparently, and compellingly to investors. A strong CFO cultivates lasting relationships founded on honesty, credibility, and consistency to maintain investor confidence.

IPO

An Initial Public Offering refers to the company's first sale of shares of stock to the public. CFOs are active participants in the IPO process, leading the preparation of financial statements, determining the company's valuation, and building confidence among investors.

J-curve

A theoretical representation of the short-term negative impact followed by long-term positive impact resulting from a new investment or business activity. The J-curve is frequently used in financial analysis to illustrate the initial costs or losses incurred from a new venture, followed by the potential for long-term growth and profitability. As CFO, understanding the J-curve can help inform investment decisions and identify potential risks and rewards associated with new business endeavors.

Job costing

A system used to calculate the precise cost of each product or service provided by a company. Job costing involves tracking labor, materials, and overhead expenses related to each job or project. For a CFO, having a strong understanding of job costing is vital, as it allows for the creation of accurate pricing models, identification of cost savings opportunities, and assessment of profitability across the business.

Job satisfaction

The level of happiness and fulfillment an employee derives from their job. Job satisfaction can be influenced by a wide range of factors, such as compensation, work-life balance, meaningful work, and opportunities for growth and development. As CFO, understanding the link between job satisfaction and employee productivity and retention is vital for creating a positive company culture and maximizing organizational success.

Joint and several liability

A legal concept in which multiple parties share equal financial responsibility for a debt or legal judgment. Joint and several liability can apply to business partnerships, joint ventures, and other collaborative arrangements. As CFO, understanding joint and several liability is important for assessing risk and exposure associated with various business relationships and financial obligations.

Joint cost

The shared cost of producing two or more products or services that cannot be easily separated. Joint costs are typically shared across products that are complementary or related in some way. As CFO, understanding joint costs is important for determining accurate product costs, forecasting profitability, and analyzing the impact of production changes and cost-saving measures.

Joint ownership

A legal concept in which two or more parties share equal ownership and control of a property or asset. Joint ownership can apply to real estate, businesses, and other types of assets. As CFO, understanding joint ownership is important for assessing potential risks and liabilities associated with a particular asset or property, as well as identifying potential opportunities for joint ventures and partnerships.

Joint venture

A type of business arrangement in which two or more companies come together to work on a particular project or venture. Joint ventures can be an effective way of sharing risk, pooling resources, and leveraging expertise to achieve a common goal. As CFO, it is important to evaluate the financial viability of a joint venture and consider the associated risks, rewards, and potential impact on the organization's bottom line.

Journal entry

A record of a financial transaction that is entered into a company's accounting system. A journal entry typically includes the date, account names, amounts debited or credited, and a brief description of the transaction. As CFO, a deep understanding of journal entries is essential for ensuring accurate and complete financial reporting, identifying errors and inconsistencies, and facilitating analysis of financial data.

Judgmental forecasting

A forecasting method that relies on expert opinion to predict future outcomes. Judgmental forecasting is often used in situations where historical data is limited or incomplete. As CFO, having a strong understanding of judgmental forecasting can help inform strategic decision-making and improve accuracy in situations where quantitative data is not readily available.

Just-in-time (JIT)

A manufacturing and inventory management system that seeks to minimize waste by producing and delivering products just as they are needed. JIT aims to streamline the production process, reduce inventory carrying costs, and increase efficiency by delivering products at the precise moment they are needed. As CFO, having a strong understanding of JIT can help identify cost-saving opportunities and improve overall operational efficiency.

Key Accounting Principles

CFOs should be well-versed in accounting principles such as the balance sheet equation, double-entry accounting, and the matching principle. This knowledge allows them to interpret financial statements accurately, make sound decisions, and communicate financial information clearly to other stakeholders.

Key Financial Ratios

CFOs should be familiar with and use financial ratios to assess a company's financial health, performance, and liquidity. Ratios such as the debt-to-equity ratio, current ratio, and return on equity can provide valuable insights into the company's financial status.

Key Performance Indicators (KPIs)

Metrics used to evaluate the success and progress of a company's financial performance. KPIs can vary depending on the industry and the company's specific goals, but examples include revenue growth, profit margins, return on investment, and cash flow. CFOs must be knowledgeable about KPIs and use them to make informed decisions that will help the company achieve its objectives.

Key Performance Measures (KPMs)

Similar to KPIs, KPMs are metrics used to evaluate the success or failure of specific projects, initiatives, or operations within a company. CFOs need to define and track KPMs to make informed decisions and continuously improve the company's performance.

Key Performance Questions (KPQs)

These are questions CFOs ask themselves when evaluating a company's financial performance, such as "What are our long-term goals for revenue growth?" or "How can we reduce our expenses without compromising quality?" Answering these questions can help CFOs identify areas for improvement and make strategic decisions.

Knowledge of Global Markets

A CFO should have an understanding of global markets and economic conditions that could impact the company's financial performance. This knowledge can help CFOs anticipate potential risks and opportunities and prepare the company to adapt as necessary.

Knowledge of Regulations

CFOs should understand and be able to comply with any relevant regulations affecting the company, including tax laws, accounting standards, and financial reporting requirements. Ignorance or noncompliance can result in legal or financial consequences, so it is crucial for CFOs to stay up-to-date and follow them.

KPI Dashboard

A visual representation of a company's KPIs that provides an at-a-glance view of performance. A CFO should be able to build and use a KPI dashboard to highlight trends and identify potential issues that need to be addressed. This information can be shared with other stakeholders in the company to keep everyone informed.

KPI Targets

Specific goals or benchmarks for KPIs that a company sets to measure progress and success. CFOs need to set realistic KPI targets that align with the company's goals and provide a clear path forward.

KPI Variance Analysis

The process of comparing actual KPIs to the targets or benchmarks set by a company. CFOs need to conduct KPI variance analysis to identify deviations from the norm and determine if these deviations are significant or not. By doing so, CFOs can determine what actions should be taken to maintain or improve performance.

Lease

A contractual agreement where the owner of an asset lends it to the lessee (a company) for a specified period in exchange for regular payments. As a CFO, understanding lease agreements is essential in making informed decisions regarding financing assets, managing cash flow, and minimizing financial risk.

Leverage

The use of borrowed funds to increase the potential return on investment. As a CFO, leveraging can be utilized to fund the company's growth or acquire new assets, but it must also be managed carefully as it can increase the company's financial risk.

Liability

Any debt or financial obligation owed by the company to external sources, such as creditors or investors. As a CFO, managing liabilities is necessary to ensure the company's ability to repay debts and maintain financial stability.

Liquidity

The ability of a company to meet its short-term financial obligations, such as paying bills and employees, with readily available cash or assets that can be quickly converted to cash. As a CFO, understanding liquidity is crucial in ensuring that the company has enough cash reserves to cover short-term needs and prevent liquidity issues that may negatively impact the business's performance.

Liquidity Ratio

A measure of a company's ability to meet its short-term financial obligations, calculated by dividing current assets by current liabilities. As a CFO, monitoring liquidity ratios assists in assessing the company's financial health and making informed decisions regarding short-term funding and investments.

Loan Covenants

Contract terms and conditions that stipulate certain requirements and restrictions for companies receiving loans from lenders, such as maintaining a certain debt to equity ratio. As a CFO, understanding loan covenants is vital to avoid default and maintain a positive business relationship with lenders.

Lockbox

A service provided by banks that allows companies to receive payments directly to a designated post office box, which is picked up and processed by the bank, ensuring faster access to funds. As a CFO, utilizing lockboxes can improve cash flow, reduce processing time, and increase efficiency in payment collection.

Long-term Debt

Any debt owed by the company that has a maturity date of over one year. As a CFO, managing and balancing long-term debt is necessary in maintaining financial stability and ensuring the ability to repay debt obligations on time.

Long-term planning

A strategic approach that involves creating a vision for the company's future and developing plans to achieve it over an extended period. As a CFO, long-term planning is essential in ensuring the company's financial sustainability and performance over time.

Loss Reserves

The funds allocated by a company to cover future losses that may occur, such as those resulting from unexpected lawsuits or insurance claims. As a CFO, understanding and managing loss reserves is essential in ensuring the company's financial stability and preparing for unforeseen events.

Management Reporting

The process of analyzing financial data and creating reports that summarize a company's financial performance. This is a critical function of a CFO role as it helps measure the company's strengths and weaknesses and allows for strategic decision making. The reports typically cover topics such as income statements, balance sheets, cash flow statements, and key performance indicators.

Market Analysis

The process of studying industry trends, customer behavior, and competitor activity to identify opportunities and risks. A CFO needs to have a solid understanding of market dynamics to devise effective financial strategies and make data-driven decisions.

Mergers & Acquisitions (M&A)

The process of combining two or more companies as a way to increase market share, economies of scale, or gain access to a new market. CFOs often play a key role in M&A deals, from negotiating terms and financing to executing the transaction and integrating the companies' financial systems.

Metric Tracking

The process of measuring and analyzing key performance indicators (KPIs) to evaluate a company's financial health and make informed decisions. The CFO is responsible for identifying relevant metrics, setting targets, tracking progress, and reporting results to stakeholders.

Multi-Year Planning

A process for projecting the financial performance of a company over a multi-year period, typically 3-5 years. This includes forecasting revenue, expenses, and capital expenditures, as well as identifying potential risks and opportunities. A CFO must have strong financial acumen and analytical skills to create accurate and realistic multi-year plans.

Net income

The amount of money a company has after deducting all expenses from their total revenue. When interviewing for a CFO role, it's important to have a strong understanding of the company's net income history and projections for the future. As a CFO, you'll need to be able to make strategic financial decisions based on this information to improve the company's financial position.

Net present value

A financial method of calculating the present value of an investment or project by considering the time value of money. As a CFO, you may use this tool to help evaluate whether a particular investment or project is a sound financial decision.

Net working capital

This is the amount of money a company has available to pay its short-term debts and expenses. As a CFO, you may be responsible for managing and optimizing the company's net working capital to ensure the organization's financial stability.

New accounting standards

When interviewing for a CFO role, it's important to have up-to-date knowledge of any new accounting standards that have recently been implemented or are in the process of being implemented. This will help you ensure that your company stays compliant with any new regulations or reporting requirements.

Non-disclosure agreement

A legal contract that prohibits one or more parties from sharing confidential information with anyone outside of the agreement. As a CFO, you may need to negotiate and sign non-disclosure agreements with vendors, partners, and other businesses to protect the company's confidential financial information.

Non-financial metrics

These are measurements that are not directly related to financial performance, but can still impact the company's success. Some examples include customer satisfaction, employee turnover rate, and website traffic. As a CFO, you may be responsible for determining how to measure and track these metrics in order to make informed financial decisions.

Non-profit accounting

This is a specialized accounting field that involves managing finances for non-profit organizations. When interviewing for a CFO role at a non-profit organization, it's important to have experience with non-profit accounting regulations and practices.

Normalized earnings

This is a method of evaluating a company's financial performance by adjusting for temporary or one-time events, such as restructuring costs or accounting changes. When interviewing for a CFO role, it's important to have experience with this type of financial analysis in order to accurately evaluate the company's financial health.

Note disclosure

A section of a company's financial statements that provides additional information about specific financial transactions or events. As a CFO, you may be responsible for drafting note disclosures and ensuring that they are accurate and compliant with accounting regulations.

Off-Balance Sheet Financing

A financial arrangement whereby a company obtains funding without reporting the debt on its balance sheet. CFOs must understand and disclose any off-balance sheet financing arrangements to stakeholders as it may impact the company's financial ratios, credit ratings, and perceived risk.

Operating Cash Flow (OCF)

A financial metric that measures a company's cash inflows and outflows from its core business operations. Having a positive OCF signifies that the company generates enough cash to cover its operating expenses and investments. It is an important metric for CFOs to analyze as it helps in assessing a company's ability to meet short-term financial obligations and fund its growth plans.

Operating Leverage

The degree to which a company's fixed costs affect its profitability. CFOs use operating leverage to assess the company's cost structure and determine the breakeven point. However, they must also consider the potential risks of having high operating leverage, including reduced flexibility and higher financial risk in the event of a downturn.

Operating Margin

A financial metric that measures a company's operating profit as a percentage of its revenue. CFOs use operating margin to evaluate the company's profitability and efficiency in generating earnings from its operations. However, they must also consider the potential impact of external factors such as changes in the industry or economic conditions on the company's margin.

Operational Efficiency

The ability of a company to utilize its resources optimally to achieve its objectives while minimizing costs and waste. CFOs play a critical role in identifying inefficient processes and implementing initiatives to increase operational efficiency. They must balance the trade-offs between cost-cutting measures and investing in growth opportunities.

Option Pool

A block of company shares reserved for employees, consultants, and directors to incentivize them to achieve corporate goals and align their interests with the company's success. CFOs are responsible for managing the option pool and determining the granting of options to individuals. They must balance the dilution effect on existing shareholders' equity and ensure the option pool size meets the company's needs.

Organic Growth

A company's growth generated through its existing operations and customers without relying on external factors such as mergers and acquisitions. CFOs must measure and monitor organic growth as it is an essential indicator of a company's long-term sustainability and potential for value creation.

Organizational Structure

The hierarchy, relationships, roles and responsibilities, and decision-making processes of a company. CFOs must understand the organizational structure and ensure it aligns with the company's goals, culture, and strategy. They must also evaluate the potential impact of any changes in the structure on the company's financial performance and stakeholders' expectations.

Outsource

The practice of hiring an external company or service provider to perform non-core functions of a company. CFOs consider outsourcing as it allows them to cut costs, optimize processes and focus on strategic initiatives. However, they must also evaluate the potential risks and consequences of outsourcing, including loss of control over certain processes, quality, and confidentiality issues.

Overall Debt Ratio

A financial ratio that measures a company's total debt as a percentage of its total assets. CFOs use overall debt ratio to evaluate the company's solvency, liquidity, and leverage. They must also balance the trade-offs between debt financing and equity financing, considering factors such as cost, risk, and investor preferences.

Payroll management

The process of managing employee compensation, including salaries, wages, and benefits. The CFO oversees the payroll function to ensure timely and accurate payment of employees, compliance with tax laws and regulations, and the implementation of effective internal controls.

Performance metrics

A set of quantitative measures used to assess the performance of a company or a specific business unit. The CFO selects relevant key performance indicators (KPIs) to track progress towards desired goals and objectives. Metrics can include profit margins, revenue growth, return on investment (ROI), or market share.

Planning and budgeting

The process of creating forecasted financial statements and a financial plan for a specific period, typically one year. A CFO prepares the budget based on the company's strategic priorities, resource availability, and expected revenue and expenses. The budget is a critical tool for managing the financial performance of the company.

Planning and forecasting

The process of creating financial projections of future performance based on historical data, market trends, and other relevant factors. The CFO uses planning and forecasting to anticipate challenges and opportunities and develop strategies to achieve the company's goals.

Process improvement

Continuous efforts to improve the efficiency and effectiveness of organizational processes. The CFO is responsible for driving process improvement initiatives by identifying areas for improvement, developing and implementing solutions, and measuring the impact of the changes.

Procurement management

The process of purchasing goods and services required for company operations. The CFO is responsible for ensuring sound procurement practices to minimize expenses and enhance efficiency. This includes developing policies and procedures for supplier selection, contract negotiation, and purchasing processes.

Product costing

The process of determining the cost of producing a product or service. A CFO utilizes cost accounting methods to identify all the costs associated with producing a product, including direct and indirect costs. The resulting cost data helps the CFO make informed decisions about pricing, profitability, and resource allocation.

Profitability analysis

Analysis conducted by a CFO to assess the company's ability to generate profits from its operations. It typically involves examining the revenue and expenses of the organization, as well as evaluating the profitability of specific products, services or business units. The results of the analysis help the CFO to make informed decisions on the financial direction of the company.

Project management

The process of planning, executing, and controlling projects to achieve specific goals and objectives. CFOs are responsible for overseeing large-scale projects, such as mergers and acquisitions, system implementations, and capital expenditures. They must ensure projects are completed on time, within budget, and meet stakeholder expectations.

Public reporting

The communication of financial information to external stakeholders, including investors, regulators, and the public. The CFO is responsible for ensuring the accuracy of financial statements, disclosures, and other financial information, and ensuring that they comply with accounting standards and regulations.

Raising Capital

CFOs often play a significant role in raising capital, whether through equity or debt financing, to fund the company's growth and operations. They must identify potential sources of capital, negotiate favorable terms, and manage cash flow to ensure the company can meet its financial obligations.

Regulatory Compliance

As a CFO, it is essential to be familiar with applicable laws and regulations that govern the company's industry and geography. Complying with regulations, such as the Sarbanes-Oxley Act (SOX) or GDPR, can be complex, and failure to comply can result in legal and financial consequences.

Reporting

As CFO, one must oversee the creation and submission of accurate and timely financial reports, including annual reports, quarterly filings, and regulatory forms. CFOs must ensure their financial reporting adheres to governing rules and regulations, is transparent, and communicates the company's financial position effectively.

Restructuring

The CFO plays a key role in restructuring initiatives, which can take several forms, including mergers, acquisitions, divestitures, or downsizing. Restructuring can have a significant impact on the company's financial statements, so the CFO must be knowledgeable about the available options, the tax implications of restructuring, and planning for value preservation.

Return of Investment (ROI)

This refers to the return that an investor may expect from their investment. ROI is vital for executives to determine the best investments and make more effective decisions in terms of capital spending, capital budgeting, and analysis for the future.

Return on Investment (ROI)

This is a financial metric used to measure the profitability of an investment. ROI measures the amount of return, or profit, generated relative to the cost of the investment. As a CFO, it is essential to calculate ROI for various investments, such as new products or expansion opportunities, to determine their viability and make informed decisions on where to allocate resources.

Revenue Recognition

This refers to the accounting principle that dictates how and when companies recognize revenue on their financial statements. As a CFO, it is crucial to have a deep understanding of revenue recognition standards, both in the US (ASC 606) and globally (IFRS 15), to ensure your company is in compliance and accurately reporting its financial results.

Risk Analysis

As a CFO, it is essential to have expertise in risk analysis to identify potential threats and opportunities that could impact the company's performance. Risk analysis involves examining the company's financials, operations, and external factors like market conditions and competitors to develop strategies that minimize risk and maximize return on investment.

Risk Appetite

As a CFO, knowing the company's risk appetite is essential for decision-making. The risk appetite is the amount of uncertainty that an organization is willing to accept to achieve its strategic objectives. Determining the risk appetite helps CFOs decide where to allocate capital, develop investment strategies, and assess investment opportunities.

Risk Management

CFOs must manage the risks that companies face daily. Risk management involves identifying, assessing, and mitigating potential threats to the company's financial health. This means developing and instituting policies and procedures that protect the company from loss, like insurances.

Sarbanes-Oxley Act

A federal law that was enacted in 2002 in response to high-profile instances of corporate fraud and accounting scandals, such as Enron and WorldCom. The act requires publicly traded companies to maintain more stringent financial reporting procedures, including independent outside auditors to verify their financial statements, the establishment of an independent audit committee, and the implementation of stronger internal controls.

SEC Reporting

Publicly traded companies are required to file periodic reports with the Securities and Exchange Commission (SEC). The CFO is responsible for ensuring that the financial statements, disclosures, and supporting documentation are accurate, complete, and in compliance with SEC regulations.

Shareholder Value

The value of a company's equity as determined by the stock price and number of outstanding shares. As a CFO, maximizing shareholder value is a primary goal, and financial decisions must be evaluated in terms of their impact on shareholder value.

Stakeholder Management

The active engagement of stakeholders, including customers, employees, suppliers, and investors, in the financial decision-making process. The CFO is responsible for ensuring that stakeholders are informed and involved in key financial decisions and that their concerns and interests are addressed.

Statutory Compliance

The process of ensuring that a company complies with all legal and regulatory requirements in the countries where it operates. The CFO is responsible for maintaining accurate and complete records of financial transactions, ensuring timely and accurate tax filings, and complying with all other financial reporting requirements. Non-compliance can result in penalties, fines, and damage to the company's reputation.

Stock Options

A type of compensation where employees are granted the option to buy company shares at a fixed price for a set period. The CFO must consider the potential financial impact of stock option grants on the company's balance sheet, income statement, and cash flow, as well as the effect on shareholder value and employee morale.

Strategic Planning

The process by which the CFO establishes the long-term financial goals and objectives of an organization. Strategic planning typically requires forecasting future revenues, expenses, and cash flows and identifying potential risks and opportunities. The CFO will work closely with executive management to set the strategic direction for the organization and develop a plan to achieve those goals.

Strategic Risk Management

The process of identifying, assessing, and mitigating the financial risks associated with achieving the company's strategic objectives. The CFO must work with executive management to develop a comprehensive risk management strategy that includes both internal and external risks and encompasses all aspects of the organization's operations.

Supply Chain Management

The management of the flow of goods and services from raw materials to finished products, including procurement, logistics, and distribution. The CFO must understand the financial implications of supply chain management decisions, such as inventory levels, transportation costs, and supplier relationships, and ensure that the supply chain is efficient and cost-effective.

Sustainable Growth

The ability of a company to grow without compromising its ability to continue to grow in the future. The CFO must balance short-term growth with long-term sustainability by managing key financial metrics such as cash flow, debt levels, and capital expenditures.

Tax Compliance

Ensuring that the organization complies with all applicable taxes and regulations is a critical duty of a CFO. Tax compliance includes staying abreast of changes in tax law and regulations, preparing tax returns, and communicating with tax authorities. The CFO must also ensure the company is minimizing tax liabilities while maintaining high ethical standards and legal compliance.

Tax Strategy

Developing a tax strategy that aligns with the company's overall business strategy is an important part of the CFO's role. This includes identifying opportunities to reduce tax liabilities through legal means, implementing tax-efficient structures for mergers and acquisitions, and staying up-to-date with changing tax laws and regulations.

Technical Accounting

Technical accounting refers to the complex accounting rules and regulations that apply to specific industries, transactions, or situations. The CFO must have a deep understanding of technical accounting to ensure accurate financial reporting and compliance with accounting standards such as IFRS, GAAP, and SEC regulations.

Transfer Pricing

Transfer pricing is the method used to determine the value of assets, services, or products transferred between different branches or entities of a multinational corporation. The CFO must ensure that transfer pricing is done appropriately to avoid tax penalties and ensure compliance with local regulations.

Treasury Management

Treasury management refers to the management of a company's financial assets and liabilities, including cash management, investments, and debt financing. The CFO is responsible for ensuring that the company has sufficient liquidity to meet its obligations, while also maximizing returns on investment and minimizing risk exposure.

Treasury Risk Management

Treasury risk management involves identifying and managing the risks associated with a company's financial assets and liabilities. The CFO must implement effective risk management strategies to minimize losses due to interest rate, currency, or credit risk.

UCC (Uniform Commercial Code)

Set of laws that govern commercial transactions, especially sales and leases of goods. CFOs must be aware of how UCC laws apply to their transactions and the impact on the company's financials.

Unaudited financial statements

Financial statements that have not been reviewed or audited by an independent auditor. CFOs must ensure the accuracy of these statements as they are used for decision-making purposes.

Underlying financial data

The fundamental data that goes into the company's financial statements. CFOs must ensure this data is accurate and reliable to make appropriate financial decisions. This includes data on revenue, expenses, assets, liabilities, and equity.

Unfunded liabilities

Liabilities that have been promised but do not have a dedicated funding source. CFOs must be aware of any unfunded liabilities, such as pensions or future medical benefits for employees, to ensure adequate funding exists.

Unit economics

A business model that takes into account the cost structure of each unit of product sold. CFOs must monitor and analyze unit economics to ensure that they have a sustainable business model.

Unsecured debt

Debt that is not backed by any collateral. CFOs must understand the risk associated with unsecured debt, including potential impacts on credit scores and the interest rate.

Us Gaap

Uniform set of accounting rules, procedures, and standards that companies use when preparing their financial statements. CFOs should have a deep understanding of US GAAP regulations, especially since public companies are required to report their financial statements using this framework.

US Treasury

The US government's department responsible for managing the country's finances. CFOs should stay up-to-date with US Treasury's policies, regulations, and economic conditions that can impact the company's financials.

User-based pricing

A pricing model where customers pay based on usage factors. CFOs should understand how user-based pricing models work, including their revenue impact and potential risks.

Valuation

Valuation refers to the process of assessing the worth or value of a company, asset, or investment opportunity. Proper valuation is essential to making informed investment decisions, and a CFO should be adept at using various methods and metrics to assess the worth of different investments or assets.

Value Chain

A value chain is the set of activities performed by a company in creating and delivering a product or service. As a CFO, understanding the value chain can help you identify inefficiencies and opportunities for improvement at every stage of the business process, from sourcing raw materials to delivering products to customers.

Value Creation

This term refers to the creation of shareholder value, which is the ultimate objective of any business. As a CFO, you need to have a strong understanding of the company's financials to identify new opportunities for revenue growth and cost-cutting, ultimately increasing shareholder value. Determining how to allocate financial resources, find new investment opportunities, and create greater efficiencies within the business all contribute to value creation.

Value Drivers

Value drivers are factors that contribute to a company's overall value, such as strong financial performance, market share, low-cost structure, customer satisfaction, or innovation. As a CFO, identifying and leveraging these value drivers can be key to generating shareholder value and ensuring sustainable growth.

Variance Analysis

Variance analysis is a method of measuring and managing the difference between planned and actual financial outcomes. A CFO should analyze the factors contributing to variation, identify specific areas of concern, and ultimately drive the company to take proactive steps to correct any factors that impact the bottom line.

Vendor Management

Vendor management refers to the process of managing and optimizing relationships with vendors and suppliers. CFOs must ensure effective vendor management to control costs, negotiate contracts, and maintain operational efficiency.

Venture Capital

Venture capital refers to capital investments made by investors or firms in early-stage companies. The effective management and allocation of venture capital financing is critical to business success in its early stages, often serving as a vital source of funding for startups and smaller companies.

Venture Debt

Venture debt refers to loans provided to early-stage companies in the start-up process, often before they have any significant revenue. As a CFO, identifying the right sources of venture debt and determining the risk-reward dynamics for each opportunity can be critical to supporting the company's growth and expansion.

Virtual CFO

A virtual CFO is a financial professional who provides all of the traditional CFO services remotely. This trend is becoming more prevalent as businesses seek to minimize overhead costs and improve the flexibility of their financial operations. As a CFO, having experience in managing virtual teams and understanding the unique challenges of this approach can be valuable in today's fast-paced and globalized business environment.

Visionary Leadership

A CFO with visionary leadership skills can lead their team forward by setting long-term goals and creating plans to achieve them. They anticipate future trends and develop strategies to take advantage of opportunities in the market.

WACC

Weighted Average Cost of Capital (WACC) is a calculation that determines a company's cost of capital by weighing the cost of all sources of funding (such as equity and debt) based on their relative contributions. As a CFO, this metric is important to understand because it can help you make informed decisions about how to finance the company's investments and operations.

Wealth Maximization

Wealth maximization is the process of maximizing shareholder value over the long-term. As a CFO, you need to balance short-term financial goals with long-term strategic planning to achieve this objective. This means making informed decisions that align with the company's overall mission and vision while also driving profitability and growth.

Weighted average maturity

The weighted average maturity is a calculation that takes the average maturity of all outstanding debt and weighs it based on the amount of each debt instrument. As a CFO, you need to be aware of this metric to ensure that the company is managing its debt appropriately and has the ability to meet its financial obligations.

Working capital

The amount of money a company has to fund its day-to-day operations. As a CFO, you will need to manage the working capital to ensure the company has enough cash to pay its bills and invest in growth opportunities. This includes monitoring cash flow, managing inventory, and negotiating payment terms with suppliers and customers. A company with inadequate working capital can run into financial troubles quickly, so it's important to stay on top of this metric.

Working capital cycle

The working capital cycle represents the time it takes a company to turn its current assets and liabilities into cash. A shorter working capital cycle is generally seen as a positive indicator of good financial management, as it indicates that the company can meet its obligations more quickly and has better cash flow.

Working capital finance

Working capital finance refers to the methods a company uses to fund its day-to-day operations. This can include short-term loans, lines of credit, trade credit, and factoring. As a CFO, you need to understand the various options available and choose the ones that work best for your company's financial situation.

Working capital management

Working capital management involves tracking and optimizing the use of a company's current assets and liabilities to ensure that it has enough cash on hand to cover its short-term obligations. As a CFO, it's your job to monitor these metrics and make adjustments as needed to maintain a healthy working capital level.

Working capital ratio

The working capital ratio, also known as the current ratio, is a metric that measures a company's ability to meet its current financial obligations. To calculate this ratio, divide current assets by current liabilities. A higher ratio indicates that the company is more financially stable and better able to meet its financial obligations.

Working capital turnover

The working capital turnover ratio measures the efficiency of a company's use of its working capital. To calculate this ratio, divide net sales by working capital. A higher ratio indicates that the company is generating more revenue per dollar of working capital, which is an indication of good financial management.

Worldwide GAAP

GAAP (Generally Accepted Accounting Principles) is the set of standards and rules that govern financial accounting in the United States. Worldwide GAAP refers to the convergence of international accounting standards into a cohesive set of principles that can be used across borders. As a CFO, you need to be familiar with both GAAP and worldwide GAAP to ensure that your financial reporting is accurate and compliant with relevant regulations.

Year-End Close

Year-end close refers to the process of finalizing a company's financial statements at the end of the fiscal year. This involves reviewing and reconciling accounts, preparing financial statements, and closing out the company's books for the year. CFOs must ensure that the year-end close is completed accurately and on time, as it impacts the reporting of the company's financial performance to stakeholders.

Year-on-Year Growth

Year-on-year growth is a financial ratio that compares a company's performance in one fiscal year to its performance in the previous fiscal year. CFOs should examine the year-on-year growth to determine whether a company is growing or declining financially while interviewing.

Years of Experience

Years of experience refers to the amount of time an individual has spent working in a specific field. While interviewing CFOs, companies often look for candidates with a minimum number of years of relevant experience as only the most competent candidate can handle the responsibilities that come with a CFO role.

Yellow Flags

Yellow flags are indicators that suggest potential problems in a company's financial performance, such as declining revenue or increasing expenses. CFOs must be able to identify and address yellow flags while interviewing as they form a vital part of an analysis of the financial health of a company.

Yield

Yield refers to the rate of return on an investment or the percentage of profits generated by an investment. CFOs should be aware of what yield is and its effect on financial planning while interviewing.

Yield Curve

The yield curve is a graph that shows the relationship between the interest rate on bonds of similar credit quality but different maturities. A CFO should be familiar with the concept of the yield curve and its implications for a business.

Yield Management

Yield management is a technique used by companies to maximize revenue by adjusting pricing based on the demand for the product or service. CFOs need to ensure that their companies are maximizing revenue through effective yield management, which involves analyzing data to determine the optimal pricing and supply of goods or services.

Yield Spread

The yield spread refers to the difference between the interest rates on two different types of securities, such as bonds. CFOs need to be well-versed in yield spreads, as they can have a significant impact on a company's borrowing and investing decisions.

Young Debt

Refers to debt that has not yet been repaid and is still outstanding. Young debt has a shorter maturity period when compared to long-term debt. It is an essential factor to consider for CFOs, as it can have a significant impact on a company's financial health, ability to borrow capital and company credit score.

YTD

YTD stands for "year-to-date," which refers to the period from the beginning of the current calendar year up to the present date. CFOs should be well-versed with YTD analysis as they guide the financial planning and analysis which is an important part of a CFO's responsibilities.

www.ingramcontent.com/pod-product-compliance
Lightning Source LLC
Chambersburg PA
CBHW071029220526
45467CB00004B/1579